Legacy in Words

Jamarica S. Jones

Order this book online at www.trafford.com
or email orders@trafford.com

Most Trafford titles are also available at major online book retailers.

Printed in the United States of America.

ISBN: 978-1-4669-7126-4 (sc)
ISBN: 978-1-4669-7125-7 (e)

Trafford rev. 05/29/2014

www.trafford.com

North America & international
toll-free: 1 888 232 4444 (USA & Canada)
fax: 812 355 4082

Contents

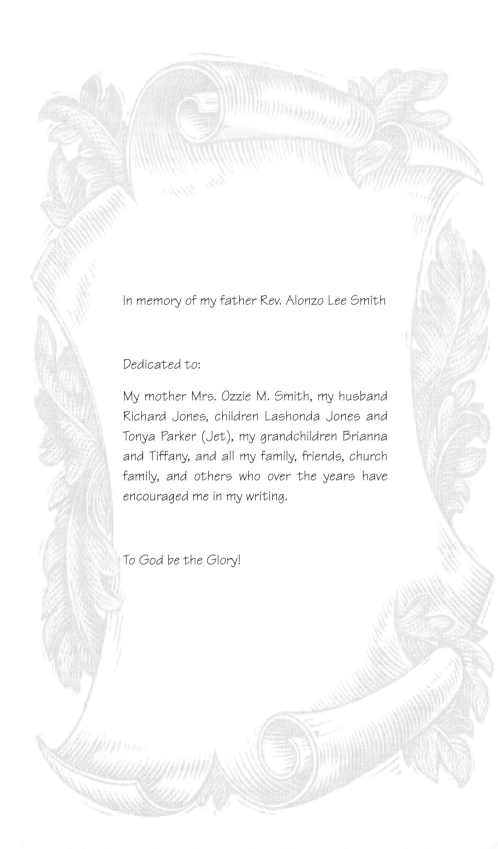

In memory of my father Rev. Alonzo Lee Smith

Dedicated to:

My mother Mrs. Ozzie M. Smith, my husband Richard Jones, children Lashonda Jones and Tonya Parker (Jet), my grandchildren Brianna and Tiffany, and all my family, friends, church family, and others who over the years have encouraged me in my writing.

To God be the Glory!

Reflection Of Life

A poem can tell of things that happen in the past,
The trials and tribulations you have had
Of things that brought you joy
And of memories you want to last.

A poem can tell of present day
How you work, how you play,
The pleasures that you hope will last
That's what you want the words to say.

A poem can tell of future dreams
Where everything is possible it seems
Of happy days and pleasant nights
Of all the things you want to be.

A poem can tell how you feel
How you love, how you live
A poem when it is written down
Becomes a Reflection of Life.

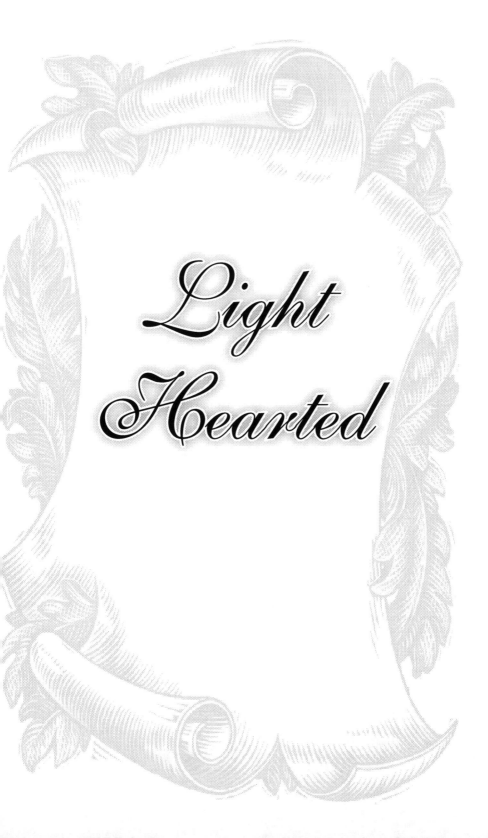

Light
Hearted

A Menopausal Moment

My patch, where is my patch?
The one that prevents my night sweats
The patch that keeps the glow from my nose,
And soothes the burn from my head to my toes.

I can be cranky without my patch
And that totally messes up my day
I'm not responsible for what I say
When I'm without my patch.

Open the windows, open the doors
Before my body heat soars
Where oh where is that patch
Look in the drawers, check all the floors.

Now, before I get real upset
Let me check, for sometimes I forget
Well, there is no more need for me to fret
My patch, Yes! I'm wearing it.

LEGACY IN WORDS

JUNK

It's amazing how quickly my house has filled
There are papers all over the table
Waiting for me to cut out a recipe or coupon
That I had totally forgotten about
Laying there on the table now it's just junk.

Then there are all the magazines
That piles up quicker than I can read.
Some were saved for their great ideas
But I did not mark the page
Now I can't remember why the idea was so great.

The closet is full of clothes
That somehow shrunk over the years
I can't bear to throw them out,
I plan to wear them again
As soon as they stretch out.

In the paper I read there is a sale,
As I gather my charge cards and money for lunch
I am off for a day of shopping.
Looking at my purchases on my return
I realize in reality, it is just more junk.

JAMARICA S. JONES

Morning Chill

I rush out of the house with only
Five minutes to get to work.
I feel the cold wind blow upon my face.
Quickly getting into the car,
I turn the key to start the motor.
Thru the window I see the sun rising
above the trees, warming the earth
and making the trees glitter in its majesty.
But the warmth had not reached the car yet.
My glasses fog when I turn on the heat.
As I sit in the car, my breath floats thru
the air like little clouds.
My body shivers from the cold.
Pulling out of the drive with
my cold hands on the steering wheel,
I think to myself, I should have
warmed this car up!

SNORE

Yes my husband snores
I must close all the doors
This snore cannot be ignored
The snore my husband snores.

If I can get him to his side
He would be just fine
But that's always a chore
He's dead weight when he snores.

He says I snore too
I know that's just not true
Women never snore
They only breathe real deep.

JAMARICA S. JONES

The Ladies At Work

The ladies at work said
Try such and such
The family at home had not heard of such
And they didn't like it very much.

The ladies at work said
Do this and that
When I tried this at home
It didn't work like that.

The ladies at work said
When you're right you're right
I tried that at home
Found they weren't right.

So I've decided
If I'm to get it right
I will ONLY listen
To the ladies at work.

Sunday Afternoon Sleep

Another Sunday afternoon resting on the sofa
with the Sunday paper and a good movie playing on the TV.
The headline boldly tells of another tragedy.
The movie is coming to an exciting scene
as my eyes close for a moment,
and the paper slips gently out of my hand.
I hear my husband's voice asking if I am sleep.
Instantly alert, I inform him that I was just resting my eyes.
I have no idea what happened on the TV.
I know my eyes were only closed for a second.
With renewed spirit, I read another paragraph,
Or had I read this one before?
The movie comes to an end
and I realize I will have to watch it again.
I refuse to believe this represents a sign of getting older.
I just stayed up too late Saturday night. Yeah right!!!

JAMARICA S. JONES

In My Pot

Peas in a pot
Peas in a pot
That's all I've got
Peas in a pot.

Carrots, carrots in a pot
Potatoes, cubed one or two
Peas, carrots, potatoes
In my pot, that's what I've got.

Ground chuck browned.
Onions, green peppers too
Not too much, just a few
Peas, carrots, potatoes, ground
Chuck, onions, peppers
That's what I've got in my pot.

Tomatoes, tomatoes in my pot
Salt, pepper, sugar just a taste,
Simmered on low, not too hot
Vegetable soup! That's what
I've got in my pot.
Dinner's ready!!

SQUIRRELS

They are everywhere
Those furry little creatures
With the long curly tails.
They find the best pecan trees,
Eating all the pecans leaving none for me.
They scurry about on top of the house
Walking the telephone lines with ease
But when they decide to cross the road
Brother you better really watch out.
Just as you start to slow down
They reverse and go the other way
Waiting until you start again,
To turn themselves completely around.
Yes, they are as cute as they can be
With their big wide eyes and wiggling nose
But they are truly a nuisance
When they eat all the pecans and cross the road.

JAMARICA S. JONES

TRAFFIC JAM

Stuck in a traffic jam
On Interstate 85
Cars and trucks bumper to bumper
Line the road in front and behind.
Creeping slowly down the road
Driving ten miles per hour at the most
I keep my foot on the brake
Trying not to drive too close.
I suppress the urgent need
For a bathroom break
I refuse to get off this road
Not even for a walk in the trees.
Finally I see a sign
That explains all this mess
One lane is closed
Two miles up the road.
Some cars continue to pass
Ignoring the merge right sign
Did they not see the flashing lights
Or read the road sign?
The song playing reminds me
That "Everything will be alright"
But here I sit biding time
In this awful traffic jam line.

Autum Of Our Lives

The autumn of our lives is ushered in with graying hair,
Bedtimes that comes before the setting sun
Evenings in front of the TV
Watching reruns that remind us of yesterday's gone.
Tired from the day's work,
We wish we had the energy of summers pass.
Our closets are full of dark clothes
That makes us look slimmer.
Our dresser drawers hold the make up
Used to cover the crow's feet
And other skin imperfections.
The bathroom holds the red hair dye
Used to bring back the color of spring.
Our cabinet drug store fails to prevent
The waking darkness of pain.
Hidden high fat foods become our secret lover.
The tight mini-skirts of our summer
Fail to cover the bulging abdomen
Or the wrinkled knees of our autumn.
Mirrors are avoided
Because they reveal the winters that are coming too quickly.
Autumn brings many changes
Including the wisdom we wished for in our summers.
No matter what we do, the seasons will change.
So let us enjoy our Autumn,
and slide gracefully into our Winter.

JAMARICA S. JONES

Monster In My Body

A monster moved into my body
I did not invite him in
His arrival was a total surprise
Now I must live with him.

He calls himself Arth Ritis
He moved into the knuckle of my right hand
But decided it was not big enough
So he quickly started to expand.

He took a day trip to my elbow
But he didn't like the bend
So he moved into my shoulder
And invited Bur Sitis to join him.

I found some special cream
To give my shoulder some relief
But Arth moved to my lower back
To a place I could not reach.

Arth is a lazy fellow
To remind me not to disturb him
He invites his cousin Pain to visit
When I go walking with my friend.

He seems now to be renting body joints
To his relatives and friends
For Inflammation, Osteo and Rheumatoid
Have all moved in.

Sometimes Arth has a party
In the middle of the night
I don't get much sleep
For no position is just right.

I hear from some of my friends
That Arth's cousins are visiting them
And they are having as many problems
As I am having with him.

Will someone please tell me
how to get these monsters out
Is there a special cream or pill
To keep them from moving about.

I don't have much money
I will pay you what I can
If you can come up
With a master monster plan.

JAMARICA S. JONES

The Big "3-0"

As a child the years seemed long
Each birthday I met head on.
By eighteen, I slowed to take a look.
Twenty one I was off my parent's hook.
Twenty five just slid right by.
At thirty now, I wonder why
The big "3-0" I did dread,
No tears will you see me shed.
The years have been good to me,
Could pass for twenty five you see.
So I will pull out that one grey hair,
Buy myself a new dress to wear,
And look forward everyday
For the big "4-0" to come my way.

ADVENTUROUS WOMAN

She claims she is older
Than the oldest dirt,
Yet she dances in the street
In her denim skirt.

Whether climbing the mountain high
Skiing down a great big slope,
Riding her bike with a flat tire,
She's always on the go.

A northern girl in a southern town
The lack of snow gets her down.
Spring temperatures of eighty eight!
Ten feet of snow would be just great.

The candy bars and potato chips
She eats between breakfast and lunch
Makes a more tasteful choice
Than the seaweed that she munch.

JAMARICA S. JONES

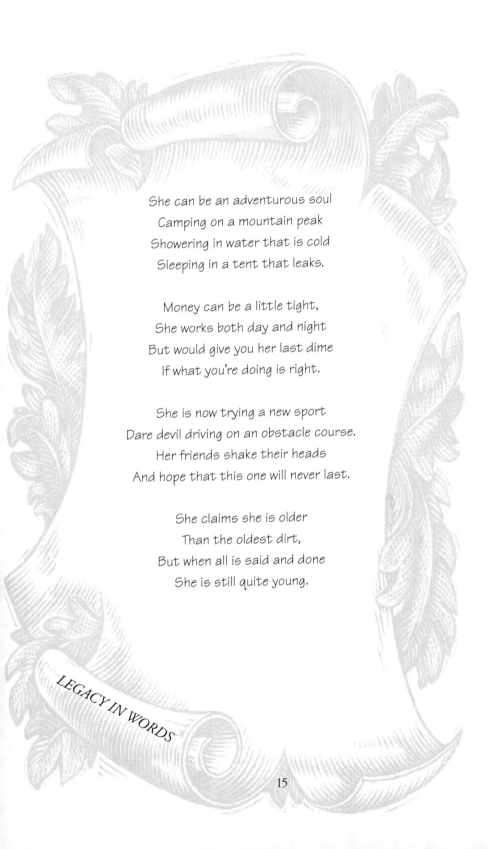

She can be an adventurous soul
Camping on a mountain peak
Showering in water that is cold
Sleeping in a tent that leaks.

Money can be a little tight,
She works both day and night
But would give you her last dime
If what you're doing is right.

She is now trying a new sport
Dare devil driving on an obstacle course.
Her friends shake their heads
And hope that this one will never last.

She claims she is older
Than the oldest dirt,
But when all is said and done
She is still quite young.

Whiskers

Whiskers is a lovely cat
Who lives in a house on a hill
He spends most of his day
Sitting in the window sill.

He watches the birds
Outside the window as they play.
And sometimes he goes out side
To chase the birds away.

He loves for you to scratch his back
And pat him on his head.
When it is time for him to sleep
He climbs onto his owner's bed.

The owners really love that cat
They can find no better way
Than to curl up with Whiskers
At the end of their day.

JAMARICA S. JONES

Caring

Hold Me Close

Hold me close
Rock me long
Before you know it
I'll be gone.

I won't be spoiled
I won't be rotten
But I'll know a love
That won't be forgotten.

Hold me close
Rock me long
The smile I'll give
Is yours alone.

LEGACY IN WORDS

Read To Me

Read to me Mama
Although I'm very young
I won't recognize the words
But I love the way your voice sounds.

Read to me Mama
I can walk around some now
Some of the things you read about
I can see them in my house.

Read to me Mama
I will be going to school soon
Help me say the word Mama
Let me make the word sounds.

JAMARICA S. JONES

Read to me Mama
When we're all alone
I don't want my friends to see
You reading to me now.

Read to me Mama
Maybe just a page
I have a date tonight Mama
And I don't want to be late.

Let me read to you Mama
As you did when I was young
Maybe you will recognize my voice
And know that I will always love you.

LEGACY IN WORDS

The Teacher Cried

The teacher cried again
As she told of her day
Told of the child she saw
That was being lost along the way.

She told of a little boy
But did not mention his name
He wanted all to think
That school was just a game.

He always joked with his friends
He became the class clown
Teachers would send him out
Just to quiet him down.

Today he had met his match
With this teacher he would not win
For she had figured it out
Written words meant nothing to him.

JAMARICA S. JONES

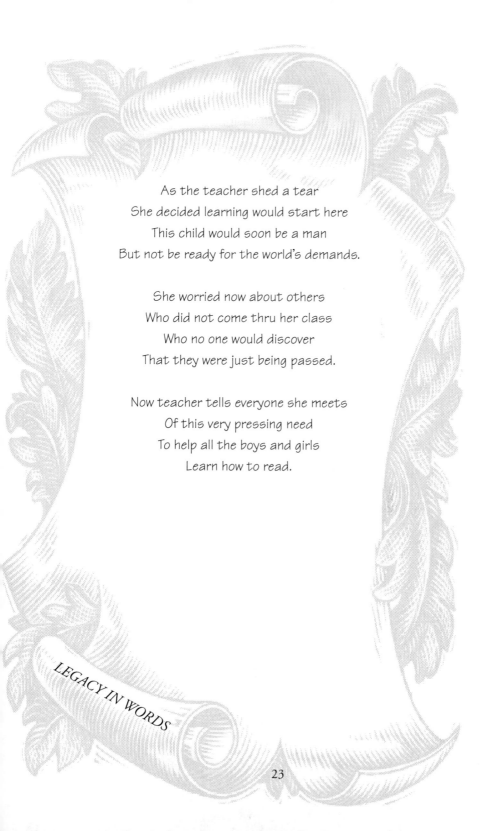

As the teacher shed a tear
She decided learning would start here
This child would soon be a man
But not be ready for the world's demands.

She worried now about others
Who did not come thru her class
Who no one would discover
That they were just being passed.

Now teacher tells everyone she meets
Of this very pressing need
To help all the boys and girls
Learn how to read.

LEGACY IN WORDS

Love

Love touches the heart
As it shines thru a smile
Whispering sweet sounds
That do not fade over the years.

Love warms the soul
It radiates from one to another
Asking only to give joy
To those who will receive.

Love overshadows any fault
Opening the mind to all possibilities
It makes differences disappear
And creates new beginnings.

JAMARICA S. JONES

Wings Of Love

You came into my life on the wings of love.
You were not flesh of my flesh,
My womb did not hold you,
But the Heavens saw fit to plant you in my heart
And my heart enfolded you with my love.

Now you are my child,
Total and complete.
Some of your actions are mine.
Words coming out of your mouth
Once were things I said to you.
You came into my life on the wings of love.
And I am glad you stayed.

LEGACY IN WORDS

GOD SENT ME YOU

I was wondering through life
Not knowing what to do
I had no goals or directions
Then God sent me you.

My days had been lonely
Before I met you
But with a touch of your hand,
I knew my love could be true.

I can't see the future
Or what it might bring,
But without you my love
It won't mean a thing.

So we stand at the altar
To pledge our love today
Together for always
We promise to stay.

With God to guide us
We will make it through,
For I truly believe
It was God that sent me you.

JAMARICA S. JONES

WHO WILL

Who will mother the mother
When she is feeling sad
Who will encourage her,
When the news is bad

Who will offer her a smile
Or a warm "how do you do?"
Who will mother the mother
When she is feeling blue

When she needs a word to guide her
Through her storm
Will you be there for her
Offer your shoulder to lean on

Who will mother the mother
Will you take on that role
Will you be able
A mother's fears to console

And who will father the father
In those lonely nights
As he ponders how
To make things turn out right

Who will father the father
When there is no money, and all the bills are due
When he receive a call
Saying, "Dad what shall I do?"

Who will father the father
Who will lend him a helping hand
Tell him not to worry
For there is a plan

Who will father the father
And who will mother the mother
Lord it's in your hand.

JAMARICA S. JONES

Family

Grandbaby In The House

There's a grandbaby in the house
She is cute and cuddly
With the prettiest little two tooth smile.
Toys are spread all around
And every room shows signs
That there is a baby in the house.
Her vocabulary is limited
But every jabbering word is understood.
The atmosphere is totally different
When the grandbaby is in the house.
Grown folks crawl around
And make happy "goo goo" sounds.
It's hard to believe
That a little one could make such a difference.
What did we ever do before
The grandbaby came into the house?

The Moody Mood

The moody mood is going around this house
Everything is met with a frown
No matter how friendly a word is said
It is very quickly shot down.

Walking on egg shells makes such a clutter
When one foot is heavier than the other
And the moody mood jumps from one to another
It's enough to make one shudder.

The moody mood just has to go
Somewhere today a smile must grow
Declaring now that some way some how
The moody mood must leave this house.

JAMARICA S. JONES

The Singer

Beads of sweat on his forehead
He sits with hands folded
The butterflies in his stomach begin to flutter
As he tries to remember the words to the song.
Standing, he looks upward
Invoking the power of the most high.
He brings the microphone to his mouth
And the melody explodes in the room
It brings tears to the eyes of the audience
As the words touch their hearts
The power of the song carries them to the mountain top
And gently brings them to the beauty of the meadow.
Completing the song, he sits down
Wiping the sweat from his brow
He commands the butterflies to be still
For truly he is The Singer.

FAMILIES

Some families are large
Some families are small
Some families talk a lot
Some families don't talk at all.

Some families live in houses
Some families are quite elite
Some families are not so lucky
They live in boxes on the street.

Some families are like clubs
Hard for you to get in
You must be extra special
Your membership to win.

Then there is the Christian family
Born form the love of Jesus Christ
Anyone can become a member
No matter where you start in life.

You can become a part of this family
Adopted into a Royal Priesthood
Just give your heart to Jesus
And move into Heaven's neighborhood.

JAMARICA S. JONES

Widow's Night

He had laid beside her for many years,
They would talk about their future,
About things they wanted to do.
They both had their spot
In a bed made for two.
Sometimes he snored loudly
Causing her to toss and turn,
And she would give him a gentle kick
To get him to turn to his side
As she would drift off to sleep
She could smell the freshness of his bath soap.
She felt the warmth of his breath
As he cuddled around her

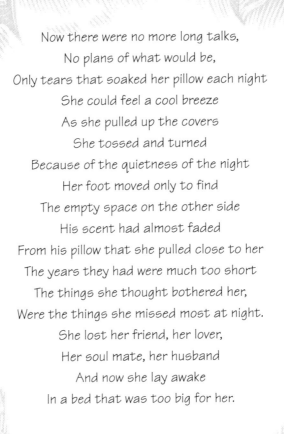

Now there were no more long talks,
No plans of what would be,
Only tears that soaked her pillow each night
She could feel a cool breeze
As she pulled up the covers
She tossed and turned
Because of the quietness of the night
Her foot moved only to find
The empty space on the other side
His scent had almost faded
From his pillow that she pulled close to her
The years they had were much too short
The things she thought bothered her,
Were the things she missed most at night.
She lost her friend, her lover,
Her soul mate, her husband
And now she lay awake
In a bed that was too big for her.

JAMARICA S. JONES

Women Who Make A Difference

You are my mothers,
Facing the struggles of life
With grace and strength
And a strong faith in God.

You are my sisters,
Daring to dream,
To reach for the stars
Asking only to be given a chance.

You are my daughters,
Walking into the future
With boldness, knowing
Just where you want to go.

You are the women in my life
Who make a difference.
Not bound by blood
But the kinship of being a woman.

LEGACY IN WORDS

It Was Our Destiny

No one would have thought
That we were meant to be
But they just did not know
It was our destiny.

The spark of love that started
So many years ago
Has grown into a fire
That burns my very soul.

Even though we don't agree
On everything we (I) do
There is one thing I know
I really, really, love you!

JAMARICA S. JONES

The Second Grandchild

When the second grandchild was born
The "oo's and "ah's" started again
A beautiful baby girl
With a heart breaking grin.

Adults are often amazed
When they talk to her
At the wisdom of an old soul
Present in one so young.

She is often found giving comfort
To the young and the old
Reassuring them without a doubt
That everything will be alright.

When this six year old prays
It brings a tear to almost every eye
And you know the prayer will be answered
As time goes by.

Now I have two granddaughters
As sweet as they can be
A great addition to our family
For they fit perfectly.

LEGACY IN WORDS

Georgia Girl

She is a strong, independent lady
The younger daughter of mine
Yet she has a tender heart
Her friends find her very kind.

She moved away from home
As children are supposed to do,
Now she is a Georgia girl
And drives like one too.

On the phone we can talk for an hour
As she tells me of things in her life
I listen with a mother's ear
And sometimes offer advice.

She has learned to face her problems
Just one at a time
So I will not worry
My Georgia girl will be fine.

JAMARICA S. JONES

Life

Beast Of The Jungle

Lie still and listen
Hear the call of the wind
Run forth, run forth, away from this jungle.

This jungle of evil thoughts
Cleanse your mind
Think of good things to come.

Gather the thoughts of your mind together
Unite for the cause, cling together as one
Fighting for a single cause.

Fight not against your fellow man
For he is for the same cause
The right to live without fear.

Cleanse your mind of hatred and greed
For the day is passing, it will soon be yesterday
And man will still not be free.

Beast of the jungle
Arise and go forth to Freedom.

LEGACY IN WORDS

The Beauty Of It All

My heart cries out again
Another family has been destroyed
Another child whose life had
Just began, was taken away
Another marriage has lost
All hope for the future

Despair, hopelessness,
Lack of love and care
So much violence and hate
That we have failed to stop and see
The beauty that is everywhere.

Hear the birds that fill the air with their song
See the golden color of the setting sun
The round white moon in the blacken sky
And the twinkling of each star
Lighting up the night.

JAMARICA S. JONES

The rainbow's colors of pink, red, yellow, and gold
Are so often missed in a world that seems so cold
The beauty of the changing trees
Is so often missed in times like these
It's time to stop!

A peacefulness could fill our souls
And love would surely grow
If we could take time to look
At the beauty of our world.

Remember

They sailed on a boat from Africa
Coming to a place called America
Crowded into a narrow hole
Many lives were lost I'm told

To a foreign country they were bought
To be sold like cattle on the selling block
Their skin was smooth and black
Except for the marks of the trader on their back.

The language they did not understand
They longed for the sounds of their homeland
In their mind they could hear the beat of the drum
At the sound, some of them would run.

To remind them of where they wanted to be
They developed song, dance, and harmony
In the master's fields they sang their song
Telling of the freedom that was yet to come

JAMARICA S. JONES

In the darkness of the night they slipped away
To the river's edge to sing and pray
A guard was placed with a watchful eye
To make sure the master did not come by.

Today we own the master's house
We can choose our own spouse
Yet some forget from day to day
To slip away just to sing and pray.

It's good to look now and then
To remember how our history began
To remember we must work and study hard to win
So that we will never be a slave again.

UNITED PEOPLE

We the people of the United States
People of many races, colors, and creeds
Living in a world of hatred and greed
We are a divided people.

We the people of the United States
Hating and killing one another
Child abused, yet no one bother
Woman killed by her own lover
A divided people.

The children shout no fear
While the Elders sit behind locked doors
Afraid to walk the street anymore
We the people of the United States
A divided people.

JAMARICA S. JONES

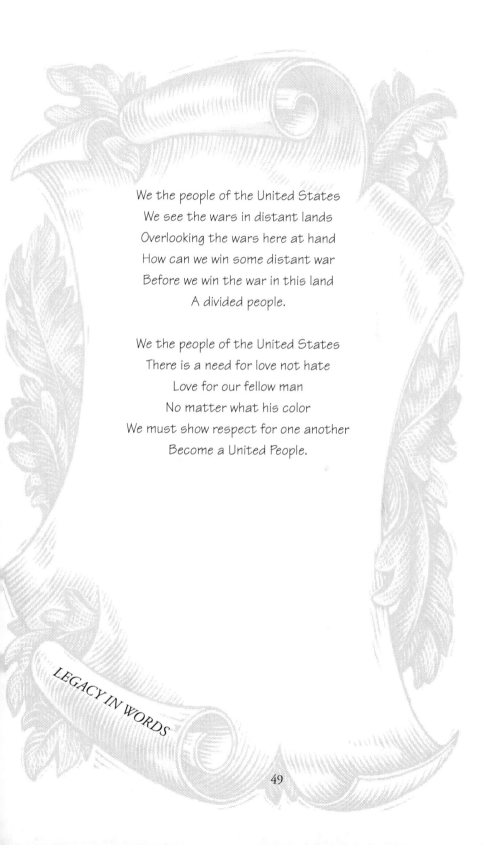

We the people of the United States
We see the wars in distant lands
Overlooking the wars here at hand
How can we win some distant war
Before we win the war in this land
A divided people.

We the people of the United States
There is a need for love not hate
Love for our fellow man
No matter what his color
We must show respect for one another
Become a United People.

LEGACY IN WORDS

SOLIDER STANDING

Solider standing in a distant land
His clothes protects him from the hot sand
He holds a gun in his hand
Fighting for freedom.

He thinks of a time when he was young
He and his friends had so much fun
Playing cowboys with a gun
He remembers freedom.

The children there have such sad eyes
No smiles, no laughter, only cries
Dodging the bullets from gun fires
Loss of freedom.

He would change things if he could
He's sadden by the loss of their childhood
He prays that their future will be good
He stays for freedom.

JAMARICA S. JONES

The Cost Of Freedom

Yesterday he was just a young boy
Graduating from high school
Getting his first new car
Trying to decide his summer plans
Talking on the phone to his favorite girl.

Yesterday she was just a young girl
Deciding what to wear to the prom
Buying a new bathing suit
Crying over an old movie
Holding hands with her favorite guy.

Today they get up with the sun
Walking miles each day
Hiding from enemy grenades
Eating food from a can
Listening to the cries of the night.

Today their dreams are changed
Nothing in their life is the same
Fighting in an unending war
Losing far too many lives
Paying much too high a price.
The cost of freedom!!

LEGACY IN WORDS

CHOOSING FREEDOM

We have freedom of speech,
Yet we are enslaved by the misuse of the spoken word
We have freedom to choose where we live,
Yet we are enslaved by the fear that comes
When someone of a different culture, or race
Moves in next door.
We are free to attend school,
Yet we become enslaved by the violence
That turns our schools from places of learning
To prisons or mortuaries.
We are free to plan for the future,
But we are enslaved because of some executives
Whose eyes and hands view their future
Above the average person.
We have freedom of opportunities,
Yet become enslaved to the drugs put in our veins
Turning opportunities into jail cells.
We are free to bear children,
Yet become enslaved when the responsibility
Of raising children conflicts with getting an education
Or a date for the high school prom.

JAMARICA S. JONES

We are free to have a wide screen TV,
But become enslaved when a child acts out
The dangers that they see
And receives broken bones, or permanent injuries.
We are free to buy guns,
But are enslaved when that gun
Is used to kill someone.
We have the freedom to be intimate
With the person of our choosing,
Yet are enslaved by the threat of AIDS.
We have the freedom to pray,
But become enslaved when we can only pray
If there is a national disaster or a lack of rain.
Today we are free to make choices,
And the choice we make will determine
Whether we remain free
Or become a Slave.

News At Eleven

Murder, robbery, high speed chase
Poison fish no one should taste
Domestic violence, license to kill
Overdose from an Oxidone pill
Child left in a hot car
While parents drink at a local bar
Homeless people walk the street
They lay under a bridge at night to sleep
Another employer moves to Mexico
Workers have no place to go
Hurricanes blow the houses down
Floods in places not usually found
Restaurants offer all you can eat
Children dying from obesity
The worse, the best and all the rest
Stations trying to pass a rating test
On the News at Eleven!

JAMARICA S. JONES

Dreams

You lay your head upon the pillow
And close your eyes to the light,
Embracing the darkness
Seeking the peacefulness of sleep
Only to be interrupted by pictures
Scrolling thru the darkness of your mind
They float by under the covers of the night
Short scenes that leave you
Pondering their meaning, their possible conclusion
A glimpse of what has been, what is now
And empty promises of what could be
They become a continuation of unspoken words
And thoughts of the day
That now become monsters in the night
Playing on the wide screen of your mind
Dreams, unexplained
They are mostly forgotten in the morning light
Yet they seem to leave a desire
To change or make different
Some part of your world
That passed under the covers of the night.
Dreams!

LEGACY IN WORDS

Is February
The Only Time I'm Black

I dress in African clothes
Watch Black history TV shows
Read about Black heroes
And learn about people who
Invented stop lights, curling irons
Peanut butter, cotton gins,
And irons to iron my clothes.

I remember a tired lady on a bus
Little girls going to Sunday school
With pretty dresses and patent leather shoes
Lives loss because someone didn't obey the rules
The story is told of people marching
And getting put in jail
But only in February.

I am reminded that it was not long ago
I would not have been allowed to vote
I see pictures of Black people sitting
In restaurants where signs read
"No Blacks Allowed"
I hear voices singing of freedom
Speakers telling about dream
But only in February.

JAMARICA S. JONES

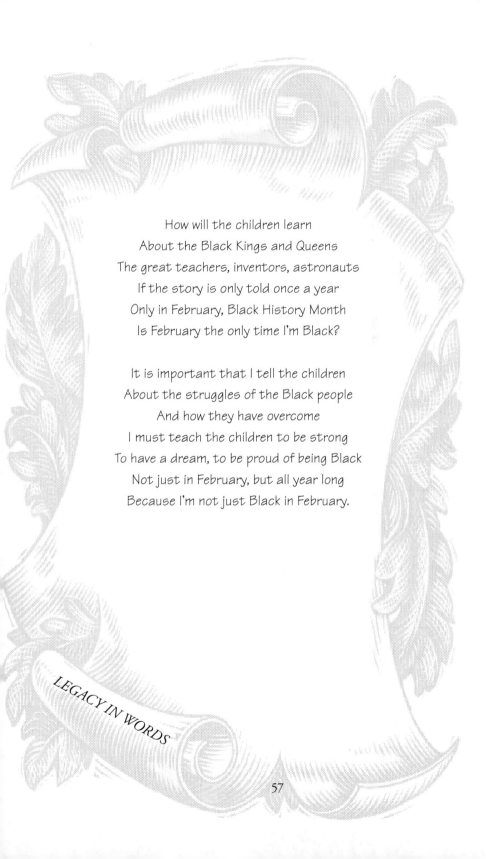

How will the children learn
About the Black Kings and Queens
The great teachers, inventors, astronauts
If the story is only told once a year
Only in February, Black History Month
Is February the only time I'm Black?

It is important that I tell the children
About the struggles of the Black people
And how they have overcome
I must teach the children to be strong
To have a dream, to be proud of being Black
Not just in February, but all year long
Because I'm not just Black in February.

LEGACY IN WORDS

New Year Resolutions

A promise to lose a little weight
By putting less on the plate
A video to exercise
In the mornings when you rise

A financial plan to save more than a dime
A promise to get to work on time
Planning to write the bills on a certain date
So they won't get there late

Resolutions made on New Year's Day
Only to be broken right away
It seems the best thing to do
Is to face each situation as it comes to you.

JAMARICA S. JONES

City Of Pleasant Living

There is danger in the streets
From sun up to sun down
You better watch over your shoulder
If you are walking in the town

Lock the doors on your car
Keep the windows closed too
Criminals break in while you are driving
Especially if your car is new

Put an alarm on your house
And keep your house closed up tight
Sleep with one eye open
In your bed thru the night

Warn all your children
To watch for strangers as they play
Be careful with relatives
If secrets are their way

The city of pleasant living
For some this may be true
But be very careful
This may not be true for you.

FLIGHT DELAY

A mighty rush to get to the right gate
A rush so we would not be late
Hoping the snow would melt away
And that there would be no delay

Aboard the plane we took our seat
Slipping shoes from our feet
Homeward bound we would surely be
At thirty minutes after three

When four o'clock came around
The plane was still on the ground
The pilot announced in Denver we would stay
There had been a flight delay

JAMARICA S. JONES

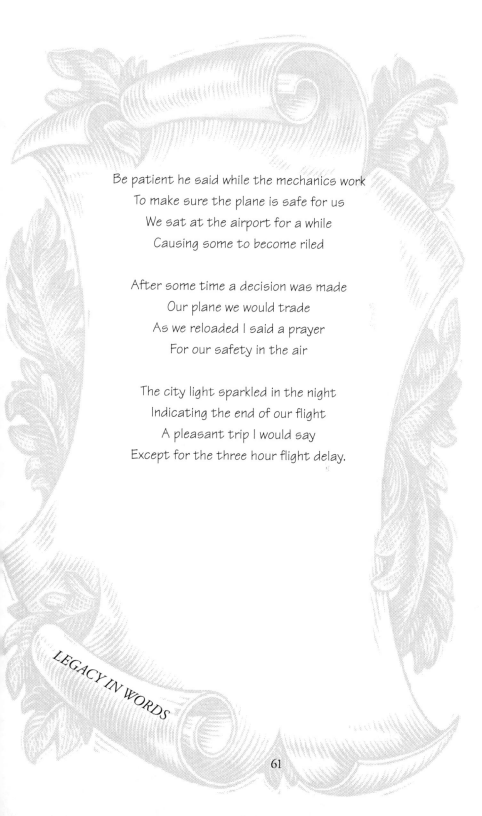

Be patient he said while the mechanics work
To make sure the plane is safe for us
We sat at the airport for a while
Causing some to become riled

After some time a decision was made
Our plane we would trade
As we reloaded I said a prayer
For our safety in the air

The city light sparkled in the night
Indicating the end of our flight
A pleasant trip I would say
Except for the three hour flight delay.

I Wait For The Day

I wait for the day when all are free
Whether red, yellow, white
Or black like me

A day when February
Is not the only time
The history of the black people
Can truly shine

A day when all the family
Sits together for a meal
Discussing the day's activities
And encouraging great ideas

I envision the day when the young and old
Are treated with respect
And the focus is on families
Not just getting what you can get

I believe with all my heart
That this dream will one day be
For things can change one step at a time
And the first step begins with me.

JAMARICA S. JONES

The Hairdresser

I know it is about time
To go to the hairdresser
For the comb halts
As it goes through my hair
And the style droops
As soon as it hits the outside air

I need her to apply
Some of those chemicals to my roots
To get out all the kinks
I want to feel her magic fingers
As they massage my scalp
Making sure the relaxer does not linger

When it is my time for the hair dryer
I will remove my shoes
And prop up my feet
Pull out a book to read
Close my eyes for a little while
Knowing I will go right to sleep

Yes, I need to go to the hairdresser
It is my special time
Not only will I get my hair done
But good conversation in between
And when I look in the mirror
I will thank the hairdresser for this new me.

A Final Goodbye

The garden was extra beautiful
Colorful flowers were everywhere
The coolness of the breeze touched their cheeks
And loosen a strand of her mother's hair

As they listen to the birds singing
It reminded her of a time years ago
When her mother would sit for hours
Watching the birds flying to and fro

The grandchildren could always make her mother smile
Seeing them caused her eyes to light up with pride
Although she was a quiet soul
Her love for them, she could never hide

Now on this very special day
As memories rushed through her head
She realized the time was close
When she would no longer sit by her mother's bed

She saw the peace upon her face
Her heart broke as a tear ran from her eye
It had been such a beautiful day
As she whispered to her mom a final goodbye.

JAMARICA S. JONES

SLOW DOWN

Bright, shiny, brand new
A gift from me to you
The car you wanted for so long
A turn of the key and you were gone

The wheels squealed as you left the drive
I felt a tear come in my eye
As silently I prayed a prayer
For your protection along the way

Slow down I whispered
Don't play the radio so loud
Never drive with a crowd
Warnings given but never heard

The road was wet late that night
As the car came into the curve
Going seventy miles per hour
On a road that was posted thirty five

The bright, shiny car was now bent
For hours your body was pent
I cried for I had not said out loud
Slow down because I Love You!

The Alzheimer Mind

The doors are locked up tight
Closed blinds cover the window
Closing out the eyes
That may be looking in

The burner on the stove is on
But nothing is cooking
Forgotten by the owner of the home
Who walked away, leaving the stove on

Keys, phones, all now gone
Stolen by that mysterious thief
Who somehow was able to get thru the door
Locks, bolts and all

Groups of people talking
Are seen as making evil plans
Throwing darts with their eyes
To destroy all that is held precious

JAMARICA S. JONES

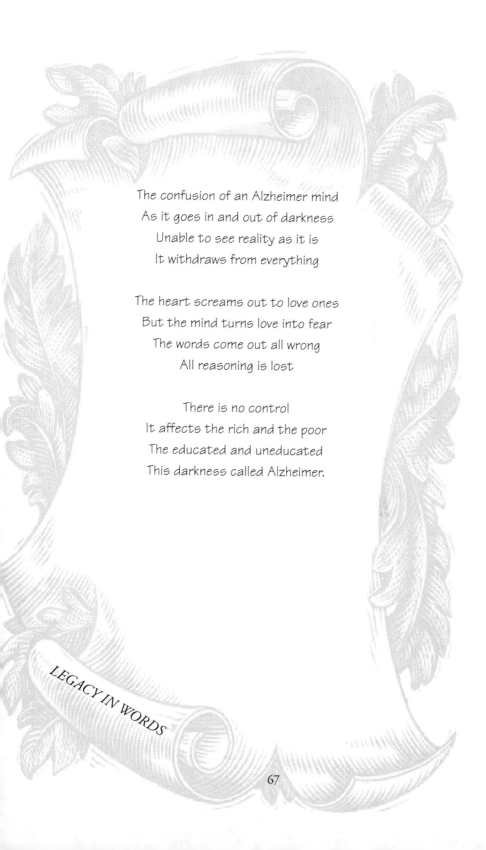

The confusion of an Alzheimer mind
As it goes in and out of darkness
Unable to see reality as it is
It withdraws from everything

The heart screams out to love ones
But the mind turns love into fear
The words come out all wrong
All reasoning is lost

There is no control
It affects the rich and the poor
The educated and uneducated
This darkness called Alzheimer.

LEGACY IN WORDS

ABUSED

She covers her face
To hide the shame that lies there
And the secrets that are beyond
The smile her lips behold.
Her arms are covered
To hide the blueness of the night,
As she searches for words
To explain the brokenness of her body.
She speaks no words
Believing that the quietness
Will cover the pain
That is within her heart.
Surrounded by family and friends
But lost in fear
Unable to find herself
Unable to escape.
Love should not bring pain or sorrow
So she is confused
By the words of love
That leads to a sharp sting on her face.
She closes her eyes
As the burn fills her chest
She drifts into nothingness
That relieves all pain
She is free.

JAMARICA S. JONES

Health

A Word For My Sister

I have a word for you my sister
One you may not want to hear
Breast and cervical cancer
Kills thousands of us each year.

This cancer can be treated
If caught early in the game
Through self-breast exams, pap smears
And yearly mammograms

Listen to the word my sister
Don't put it off again this year
There would be such an empty space
If you my sister were not here.

Little Baby

Little baby born so new
Must I get a shot for you?
I know that it will prevent disease
But how can I give you ease?

Little baby born so new
To show my love this I must do
Get regular Well Checks for you
And yes, get your immunizations too.

JAMARICA S. JONES

Track Walking At Sunrise

Come my friends let's walk the track
Men in front, women in back
We each can have a separate lane
And even a parking space to claim.

Don't wait for Betty Crocker to cook
Don't worry about how you look
But please cover up that bed head
Or the birds may nest there instead.

We won't pet the stray black cat
With the white line down its back
Let's avoid any fragrant perfume
At least until late afternoon.

Yes, we have a few romantic gents
Who with the greatest of intent
Court their wives on Valentines
With sparkling hearts and chocolate mints.

We'll not be serious all the time
When there is so much laughter deep inside
Especially when we hear such tall tales
Of little shaggy dogs and big grizzly bears.

Now we won't walk if it is real cold
Nor in heavy rain we're much too old
Those days we can sit and relax
On the carport in the back.

The new girl we will welcome in
To share good times among friends
Warning her of the rock showers from the stands
Hoping they will never come again.

Two of us will keep track
Of the laps we walk around and back
With twelve pennies we will begin
Ending also with twelve not ten.

Come my friends let's walk the track
It will make us healthier that is a fact
But a special friendship will be the best prize
Track walking at sunrise.

JAMARICA S. JONES

Beach/
Nature

Shadow Boxing On The Beach

From a distance one could see
A tall dark young man
Dancing up and down in the sand
In his black and white pants on the beach

His body appeared in perfect rhythm
As he punched with his arms and hands
The exercises were not unique
They came easy for this young athlete

Going thru his routine
Prancing, stretching, dancing
Unaware of the people passing
Who glanced his way as they go by

Then his exercise complete
He strolls gracefully on
Knowing that he is a winner
Shadow boxing on the beach.

The Beach

Seashells lying in the sand,
People walking hand in hand
Children making lots of plans
To build sand castles in the sand

White waves rushing with such force
On no particular course
Seems to play a game of tag
With those brave souls who dare to lag

Birds flying way up high
The ocean seems to touch the sky
Pleasant memories we will keep
Of our visit to the beach.

JAMARICA S. JONES

Pink Rose On The Fence

A single pink rose
Standing by the rustic old fence
Seems to stand guard
At the fork of the road

While the trees all around
Turn gold, yellow and brown
The rose flounce its color of pink
On that old rustic link

The rose will soon fade away
Its petals blown by the wind
Many who have passed this way have missed
The beauty of the pink rose on the rustic old fence.

The Moon Smiled

Oh what a busy day
All the hard things came my way
The telephone rang off the hook
There were problems every where I looked.

At home there was no slowing down
I was met with a big frown
Because dinner was not ready yet
And the dog needed to go to the vet

As I prepared to go to bed
I tried to gather some peace within my head
Glancing out the window I did see
The moon smiling just for me

Instantly I knew things would be alright
I would sleep peacefully thru the night
And when I would awake in the morning light
I would remember the moon smiled at me last night.

JAMARICA S. JONES

A Christmas Snow

Can you believe a Christmas snow
Only seen so long ago
But the newsman promises there will be
A Christmas snow this year to see

The flakes are big as they fall down
Covering quickly all around
A blanket of white covers the street
Everyone shouts out with glee

The children run outside to play
Getting out their brand new sled
From the highest hill they go
Faster, faster on the snow

Just a few snowball fights
Snow angels take their flight
Snowmen with a carrot nose
Oh what fun this Christmas snow.

Short and Sweet

Time

My Sweetheart gave me a Valentine
The words inside all rhymed
The big red heart on the front was sweet
But nothing could ever beat
The special times with
That Sweetheart of mine.

Night To Day

Moon light
Shining bright
Providing light
Throughout the night
Until the morning sun
Shines its light
On this world's plight
Day is dawn.

JAMARICA S. JONES

Apple Pies

He stood in the doorway
Watching as she picked the apples.
She had waited patiently
Since the first blooms appeared
For the apples to start falling.
The memory of her apple pies
Caused his taste buds to tingle,
She made the best apple pies.
Walking swiftly out to the tree
He helped her to fill her basket
Anticipating a sweet dinner treat.

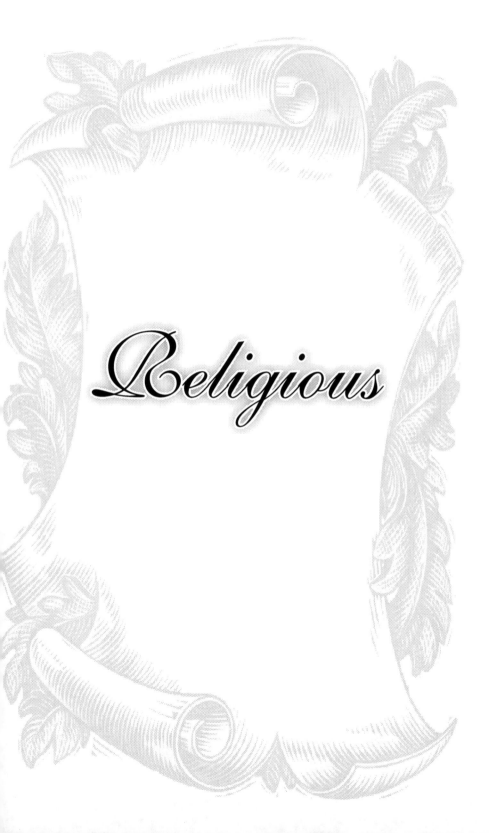

Religious

BLESSED

Sometimes in life the road seems rough
It happens to the best of us
Maybe it's all just a test
To help us remember that we are blessed

There are times the nights seem long
The struggle at its worst
It is then that God comes to us
He gives us peace and makes us strong

We must keep the faith
As we face each new test
Knowing God will guide us thru
Showing us just what to do
We are BLESSED.

Don't Play For Me
No Sad Song

Don't play for me no sad songs
When I have gone to my heavenly home
Play music with beats that soar
As I enter Heaven's door.

Wear dresses of purple, green and gold
Give praises to the God that saved my soul
Be happy as you can that day
Even though I have gone away.

Try to remember the pleasant times
And forgive me for the bad times
It does not matter what else you do
The rest is completely up to you
But please, don't play for me no sad song.

JAMARICA S. JONES

PREACHER MAN

Preacher Man, oh Preacher Man
Telling a wondrous story over again
Of a Savior who died upon a tree
To set a poor sinner free.

Preacher Man, can you take a rest,
After all you have been very blessed?
Too many souls you say yet to set free,
I cannot take a rest now you see.

A long white robe and a golden crown
For the Preacher Man is Heaven bound
There at the Savior's feet to rest
Knowing within he has done his best
Preach on Preacher Man, Preach on.

Sunday Morning Christian

I will be a Christian on Sunday morning
Have to go to work early on Monday
Working all day long with those mean folk
I cannot be a Christian and win their vote.

Why should I go to Bible Study on Wednesday night?
Those people there stay too long,
I can read my Bible here at home
I cannot be a Christian on Wednesday night.

No, I cannot go on Saturday to witness
That is the day I take care of business
Have to make preparations for Sunday church
Being a Christian on Saturday is asking too much.

JAMARICA S. JONES

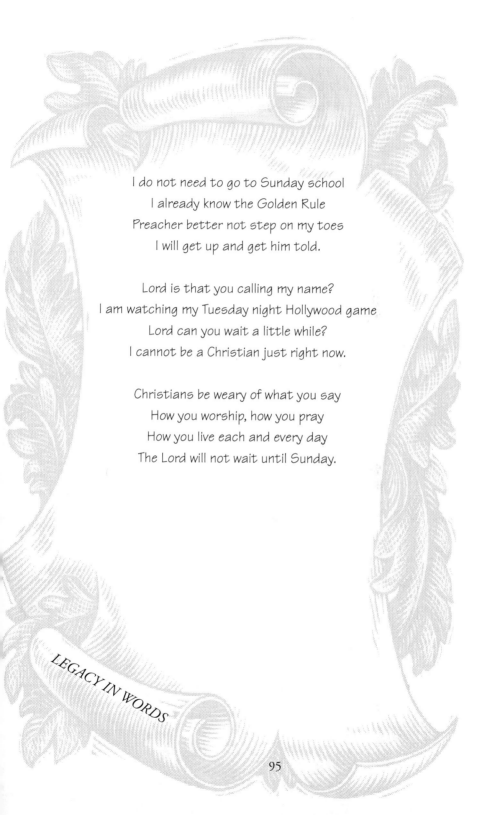

I do not need to go to Sunday school
I already know the Golden Rule
Preacher better not step on my toes
I will get up and get him told.

Lord is that you calling my name?
I am watching my Tuesday night Hollywood game
Lord can you wait a little while?
I cannot be a Christian just right now.

Christians be weary of what you say
How you worship, how you pray
How you live each and every day
The Lord will not wait until Sunday.

Thank You God

Thank you God for our families
As they gather on this day
They could be many other places
But they chose to come this way.

There were many family blessings
That we received throughout the week
We pause now to thank You God
Your continued blessing we do seek.

Let Your presence be felt today
In everything we do
Through our worship and our praise
May we show our love for You.

As our family leaves this place
We ask Your protection along the way
And may they carry just a little joy
From worshiping here today.

JAMARICA S. JONES

Special Gift

I wish for you a special gift
For this Christmas season
You cannot buy it at the mall
Or from the Christmas catalog.

Santa cannot bring it
In a red bag on his sleigh
Money cannot buy it
And you cannot put it on lay-a-way.

You won't have to exchange it
For the size and color is just right
No one can ever steal it
Once given, it is yours for life.

You must open your mind to receive it
And in your heart believe it
This special gift for you,
Is the gift of Jesus Christ.

LEGACY IN WORDS

Heaven's Chariot

You heard the Angels singing
Sweet music in your ear
Drawing you closer to Jesus
The one you loved so dear.

Torn between earth and heaven
You lingered for a while
Though you were tired and weary
You had a heavenly smile.

When you could no longer tarry
In this world here below
God sent His heavenly chariot
And to Heaven you did go.

Our hearts will be sad and lonely
At times we will shed a tear
But we will always love you
And your memory we will hold dear.

JAMARICA S. JONES

Author Biography

Jamarica S. Jones is married to Richard Jones.

She is the daughter of the late Rev. Alonzo L. Smith and Mrs. Ozzie M. Smith

She is the mother of Lashonda Jones and Tonya J.Parker (Jet)

She is the grandmother of Brianna Miller and Tiffany Parker

The author graduated from Gardner-Webb College in 1972 with an Associate Degree in Nursing.

She worked as a Public Health Nurse with the Cleveland County Health Department in Shelby NC in the Child Health Clinic for 35 years, retiring in 2010. She is an active member of the New Ellis Chapel Baptist Church in Shelby NC. Her hobbies include making Christmas Snowmen and Angel ornaments.

The author writes poems about things that happen in the everyday world, things that she sees, hears and feels. Some of her poems tell of her hopes, dreams, fears, victories, and faith. The poems may not always be based on the author's personal experiences, but are the experiences and responses of others expressed in a personal way. They are written so that anyone reading them will identify themselves or someone they know.

Other publications include: Poem—"Mother within Me" Treasured Poems of America

Poem—"Excuse Me Young Man" Firefiles and June Bugs—Down-Home Stories And Poems

Fictional Essay—"Winter Snow" Hearts and Minds of Cleveland County